Hola,
MEXICO

by Leah Kaminski

CHERRY LAKE PUBLISHING · ANN ARBOR, MICHIGAN

Published in the United States of America by Cherry Lake Publishing
Ann Arbor, Michigan
www.cherrylakepublishing.com

Reading Adviser: Marla Conn MS, Ed., Literacy specialist, Read-Ability, Inc.

Book Design: Book Buddy Media

Photo Credits: ©13spoon/Getty Images, 30 (background), ©Adalberto Rios Szalay/Sexto Sol/Getty Images, 10 (bottom), ©Aurora Open/Getty Images, 12, ©EddieHernandezPhotography/Getty Images, 44, ©EyeEm/Getty Images, 29 (top), ©ferrantraite/Getty Images, 13, ©Filippo Manaresi/Getty Images, 24, ©filo/Getty Images, background, ©fitopardo.com/Getty Images, 16, ©fitopardo.com/Getty Images, 22, ©fitopardo.com/Getty Images, 35, ©fitopardo.com/Getty Images, 38, ©g01xm/Getty Images, 21 (top), ©Gabriel Perez/Getty Images, 25 (bottom), ©Gabriel Perez/Getty Images, 31, ©Hill Street Studios/Getty Images, 27, ©iStockphoto/Getty Images, 3, ©iStockphoto/Getty Images, 6, ©iStockphoto/Getty Images, 17, ©iStockphoto/Getty Images, 21 (bottom), ©iStockphoto/Getty Images, 26, ©iStockphoto/Getty Images, 28, ©iStockphoto/Getty Images, 29 (bottom), ©iStockphoto/Getty Images, 33, ©iStockphoto/Getty Images, 39, ©iStockphoto/Getty Images, 40, ©iStockphoto/Getty Images, 45, ©Lawrence Goldman Photography/Getty Images, 9, ©LightCapturedByDamian/Getty Images, 1, ©Luis Diaz Devesa/Getty Images, 14, ©Maria Swärd/Getty Images, 8, ©Marilyn Angel Wynn/Getty Images, 42, ©Matt Mawson/Getty Images, 5, ©Mint Images RF/Getty Images, 30, ©Monica Rodriguez/Getty Images, 34, ©Pedro Mera/Getty Images, 18 (top), ©Priscila Zambotto/Getty Images, 25 (top), ©RapidEye/Getty Images, 4, ©Sandy Huffaker/Getty Images, 19, ©stockcam/Getty Images, 20, ©Susana Gonzalez/Getty Images, 7, ©Susana Gonzalez/Getty Images, 37, ©Tetra images RF/Getty Images, 11, ©Westend61/Getty Images, 23, ©EFE/Mario Guzmán/Newscom, 18 (bottom), ©3506782/Pixabay, 41, ©MiguelRPerez/Pixabay, 36, ©Dreamframer, Shutterstock, 10 (top), ©Marcos Castillo, Shutterstock, 43

Library of Congress Cataloging-in-Publication Data has been filed and is available at catalog.loc.gov

Cherry Lake Publishing would like to acknowledge the work of The Partnership for 21st Century Learning.
Please visit www.p21.org for more information.

Printed in the United States of America
Corporate Graphics

TABLE OF CONTENTS

CHAPTER 1

WELCOME TO MEXICO!

The Aztec civilization thrived in the 15th and 16th centuries. It is known for its rich culture, mythology, and artwork.

Estado Unidos Mexicanos, or Mexico, is one of Latin America's most important countries. Mexico's tropical south is filled with **pre-Columbian** ruins. Huge ranches spread throughout the dry north. Its people live in packed cities and in quiet villages. Mexico is a diverse, vibrant country defined by its variety.

The Mexican culture is a combination of its **indigenous** and European roots. Indigenous cultures like the Maya and Aztec made up the population of Mexico until the early 16th century when Spain **colonized** the country. It became free from Spain in 1821, changing its name from New Spain to Mexico. Today, the culture of Mexico is a blend of both ancient and European influences.

The agave plant grows in dry regions of Mexico. Agave is used to make certain drinks and sweeteners.

ACTIVITY

Mexico is bordered to the east and west by large bodies of water. Using a separate sheet of paper, trace the map of Mexico. Include these bodies of water on your map: the Pacific Ocean, the Gulf of California, the Gulf of Mexico, and the Caribbean Sea. Mexico also has two major peninsulas. A peninsula is a piece of land that extends out from a larger landmass into a body of water. Be sure to label Baja California and the Yucatán Peninsula. Which bodies of water border Baja California? Which bodies of water touch the Yucatán?

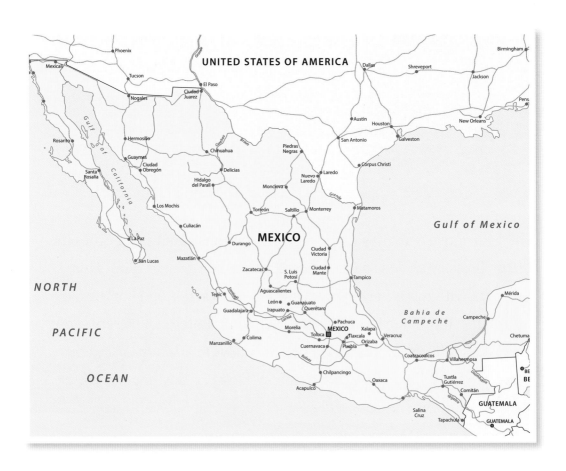

The Popocatépetl volcano, known as "Popo," is located in the State of Mexico, close to Mexico City.

The 14th-largest country in the world, Mexico is about three times the size of Texas. Mexico is part of what's called the "Ring of Fire." This is an area with many earthquakes and volcanoes. It has many rugged mountains, too. The Sierra Madre Oriental mountain range runs along the eastern side of the country. The Sierra Madre Occidental and the Sierra Madre del Sur run down the west. Between the ranges is a high plateau called the Mexican *altiplano*, or high plain. It is also referred to as the central plain. Mexico City is on the *altiplano*.

The El Chiflón waterfalls can be found in Mexico's tropical south.

Tropic of Cancer

The Tropic of Cancer is the name for the most northern **latitude** where the sun can be directly overhead. It divides Mexico's northern and southern climates. South of the Tropic of Cancer is considered the tropics, and north is the **temperate** zone.

Mexico's climate is dry and temperate in the north and tropical in the south. Its climate is diverse because of its mountain ranges and the oceans on both sides of the country. Weather along the coasts is hot and humid. Inland communities at higher elevations, such as Chihuahua and Mexico City, are drier. Some high mountain areas can even reach freezing temperatures in the winter.

The Sonoran Desert covers 120,000 square miles (310,800 square kilometers) across northwest Mexico and the southwest United States.

The animal and plant life of the Rio Grande, which forms the border between Mexico and Texas, suffers from human activity, including disruption from dams, water taken for agriculture, and pollution.

Deforestation

Mexico has the fifth-worst **deforestation** rate in the world. Deforestation leads to soil erosion and flooding. It is also a major cause of climate change. Cattle ranching and growing cities increase deforestation. Avocado farming is also a major new factor in Mexican deforestation. **Ecotourism** is one way that Mexico is trying to save its forests.

Mexico's major environmental problems come from population growth, agriculture and ranching, and **industrialization**. One urgent issue is that clean water is hard to find. People in Mexico's growing cities are using too much water from aquifers, or underground reserves of water. Overuse leads to cracks in the aquifers. They become poisoned by dangerous chemicals. Water is also polluted by farming chemicals, animal waste, and untreated sewage. This means many Mexicans must use expensive bottled water at home.

Water is becoming hard to find, too. After 500 years of use, Mexico City's aquifers are becoming so empty that the land and buildings are actually sinking. Droughts caused by climate change have reduced the supply of water even further.

Another problem in Mexico City is smog. Because of the extremely high population, Mexico City recently had unhealthy and polluted air. It is improving, though, through measures like "No Drive Days" (*Hoy No Circula*).

Monarch Butterfly

In winter, you can see flocks of 100 million monarch butterflies that have migrated south to Mexico. This beautiful orange-and-black butterfly is threatened by **habitat loss** in both the US and Mexico. The population has declined by over 80 percent. In protected areas of Mexico, human actions like illegal logging and farming threaten them. In late 2018, the US federal government began plans to construct a US-Mexico border wall through an important monarch habitat in Texas.

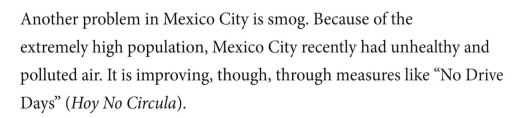

Scarlet macaws are considered one of the most intelligent species of birds. People claim macaws are as smart as 8-year-old humans!

Mexico's ecosystems are diverse. They include rain forests, deserts, and prairies. Mexico holds over 10 percent of the Earth's plants and animals. Over one-third of its animal species are endemic, which means they only exist in Mexico. Many of these species are threatened. Mexico is one of the countries with the highest number of threatened mammal species.

CHAPTER 2

BUSINESS AND GOVERNMENT IN MEXICO

Mexican adults work in many types of jobs. About 13 percent work in agriculture, 24 percent manufacture goods, and 62 percent provide services. This means they sell their time, effort, and ideas. One important service in Mexico is tourism, which includes jobs like hotel workers and travel agents.

Mexico has a great number of independent bakeries. Many families have run their bakeries for generations.

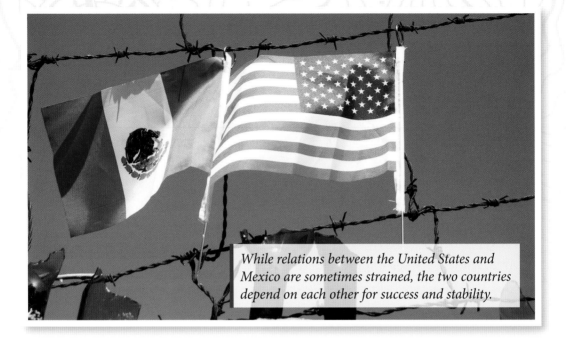

While relations between the United States and Mexico are sometimes strained, the two countries depend on each other for success and stability.

Mexico's relationship with the United States is important to its economy. About half of Mexican **imports** come from the United States. Nearly four-fifths of Mexican **exports** go to the United States. The United States relies heavily on Mexico for **petroleum**. Mexican workers in the United States and elsewhere send a lot of money home. Mexico makes more money from this than from tourism or petroleum exports.

NAFTA

NAFTA stands for North American Free Trade Agreement. It is an economic agreement between the United States, Mexico, and Canada. Signed in 1992, NAFTA gets rid of most tariffs, or taxes, on goods traded among the members. A new agreement called the United States–Mexico–Canada Agreement (USMCA), or New NAFTA, was signed in late 2018. The US Congress plans to vote on whether to ratify it in 2019.

A key part of Mexico's economy is the *maquiladora*. *Maquiladoras* are factories owned by foreign companies. Many are near the United States border, run by United States companies. Materials are brought into Mexico and assembled into products to be exported. In 2013, *maquiladoras* made 65 percent of Mexican imports.

MEXICO'S IMPORTS AND EXPORTS

Do you want to know more about Mexico's economy? Take a look at its trading partners. Trading partners are the countries that import goods from a country or export goods to that country. Here is a graph showing the countries that are Mexico's top import and export trading partners.

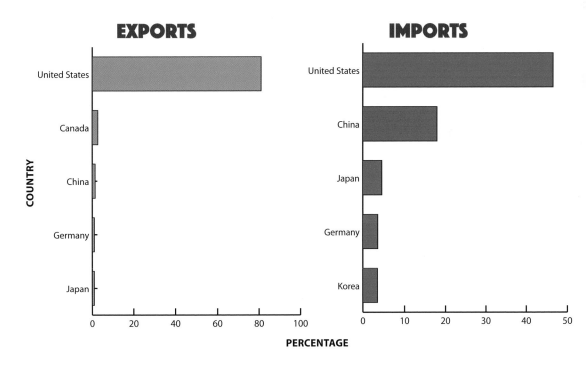

The people of Mexico have been farming maize and corn for about 10,000 years.

Mexico has ancient farming traditions, but it also has a modern farming industry. Agriculture's role in the economy is shrinking. Mexico now imports more of its agriculture than it produces.

Corn is one of Mexico's most important crops. Because of drought in northern Mexico, the growth of corn has dropped and now Mexico is one of the largest importers of corn in the world.

Cartels

Mexican drug **cartels** sell and move drugs between countries in South and North America. In 2017, almost 30,000 people died in violence related to this illegal drug trade. The violence is only growing. Shootings have occurred in popular tourist destinations recently, from Acapulco to Cancun. President Andrés Manuel López Obrador has vowed to stop the violence by fixing the social problems that lead people into crime.

Cattle graze along more than 80 percent of the land in Mexico's northwest state of Sonora.

Livestock makes up about 30 percent of Mexican agriculture. Ranching is an important tradition in northern Mexico. During Spanish rule, there were many huge *haciendas*, similar to plantations. These were broken up after the Mexican Civil War, but there are still many cattle ranches.

Andrés Manuel López Obrador was inaugurated as president on December 1, 2018, in Mexico City.

Mexico is a democratic republic. Just like the United States, the Mexican government has three branches led by a president. The current president is Andrés Manuel López Obrador.

Women in the Government

In Mexico, 50 percent of a political party's **legislative** candidates must be women. After the 2018 election, women held one-half of national legislative positions. Mexico is now the only country with a majority female Senate. To compare, nearly a quarter of legislators in the United States are women.

Migrant Workers and the Border Wall

At the beginning of 2019, US troops fired tear gas into a group of **migrants** entering the US from Tijuana, Mexico. Seeking **asylum** from all over South America, they camped in Tijuana for a month before this attack. There is growing controversy about Central American immigration through Mexico. Disagreement between pro-immigrant and anti-immigrant Americans is strong. President Donald Trump is anti-immigration and wants to build a border wall between the two countries.

The National Palace is the president's official seat of power, like the White House in the United States.

Mexico is made up of 31 states plus the Federal District. The Constitution of 1917 was written after the Mexican Civil War, which caused big changes to the government. The Constitution guarantees rights to Mexican citizens. All Mexican citizens age 18 and older are required by law to vote.

The President and their cabinet make up the executive branch. The president holds most of the power in the government. Presidents can only serve a single 6-year term.

The National Palace holds the offices of the president, the treasury, national archives, and a parliamentary chamber.

Most serious legal cases are heard in federal courts with a judge but no jury. Courts and prisons in Mexico have had problems with long wait times and overcrowding. This creates unfair situations, especially for poor indigenous people.

The legislative branch is the Senate and Chamber of Deputies. There are 500 Deputies and 128 Senators. No consecutive terms are allowed.

CHAPTER 3

MEET THE PEOPLE

There are an estimated 130 million people living in Mexico today. Nearly two-thirds of them are *mestizo*. This means their **heritage** is a mix of indigenous and Spanish. Another nearly 30 percent are indigenous or mostly indigenous. The other 10 percent are of European heritage. Mexico's foreign-born population makes up less than one percent of the population. This number is growing, though. The largest group of immigrants are from the United States, including those whose family origins are Mexican.

Mexico City covers almost 600 square miles (1,600 square km), which is about the same size as Houston, Texas.

Mexico's official language is Spanish. There are also dozens of recognized indigenous languages. More than 1.5 million Mexicans speak an indigenous language called Nahuatl.

Eighty percent of the population now lives in cities. Mexico City is one of the most crowded cities in the world. However, cities do not control the country's culture. Rural communities are very attached to their *patrias chicas*, or small homelands. These communities often have their own languages and customs. This helps protect the country's cultural diversity.

Mexican folk dance features lively music and bright costumes.

The Metropolitan Cathedral of Mexico City took over 240 years to build. It was finished in 1813.

Pre-Columbian Mexican cultures were complex and city-based. They supported arts, architecture, and science. Hernán Cortés came from Cuba in the early 1500s to colonize these cultures. He was helped by his stronger technology and **epidemics** of new diseases that weakened the locals. After Cortés overcame the indigenous people, Mexico City was built over the ruins of the Aztec capital. In New Spain, only Catholicism was allowed.

Lands rich in silver have led to a great variety of jewelry in Mexico.

The impact of the Spanish on the region survives to this day. However, 500 years after the arrival of the Europeans, Mexican indigenous groups have kept their own identity. *Indigenismo*, or pride in indigenous heritage, has been an important idea in Mexico since the 1930s. The government supports folk arts and crafts along with the European-inspired classical arts. Mexican indigenous peoples still practice ancient craft traditions of silver work, pottery, mosaic, and basket weaving.

La Charreada

La Charreada is a sport similar to rodeo. Dating back to the 16th century, it preserves *charro* (cowboy) traditions. The *charros* perform in events like bull riding and roping. The outfits and equipment are made by local craftspeople. Some states have recently begun to ban bull-related events because the bulls are mistreated.

Do you live in the United States? If so, there is a good chance that you have classmates or friends with cultural ties to Mexico. You may even be Mexican or Mexican American yourself. It would take another book to cover the rich history that links Mexico to its northern neighbor. They share indigenous cultures, they have fought wars against each other, and more. Would you like to learn more about the cultural and historical ties these countries share? Try some independent research—ask a librarian to help you find books and other resources on these topics.

While guacamole has been a part of Mexican cuisine since the 1500s, it didn't reach the United States until the early 1900s.

Many parts of Mexican culture are celebrated in the United States. One example is piñatas *at birthday parties.*

Mexico has many local art forms with pre-Columbian roots. For example, in *mariachi* bands, musicians play trumpet, violin, and two types of guitar while wearing *charro* costumes. Muralism, the most important 20th-century Mexican art form, also has indigenous ties. In the early 20th century, Diego Rivera and others painted the political life of the Mexican Civil War in large, colorful murals. Of course, Mexicans also enjoy modern entertainment, like soap operas (*telenovelas*). Some popular recent Mexican *telenovelas* are *La Reina del Sur* and *Maria la del Barrio*. Soccer (or *futbol*) is the most popular sport in Mexico.

Large murals can be found in many cities and towns across Mexico. Many tell stories of past events.

In Mexico, many artisans create their crafts—such as pottery, weaving, and woodwork—by hand.

CHAPTER 4

FIESTAS

Many of Mexico's holidays and festivals, called *fiestas*, are Catholic. Carnaval (a festival before Lent), Easter, and Christmas are among the most important. *Las Posadas* takes place the week before Christmas and was created by Spanish **missionaries**. There are also many local festivals for patron saints. The holiday Mexico is most known for is *Día de los Muertos*, or Day of the Dead. This takes place the day after Halloween.

The Day of the Dead is celebrated across Mexico, as well as in parts of Central and South America and the United States.

There are fun personal celebrations, too, like birthdays. Mexican birthday parties feature great food, singing, and *piñatas* loaded with goodies. In Mexico, people also celebrate what is called a name day or a saint's day. Children are sometimes named for a Catholic saint, and each saint has a "saint's day," on which people with that name celebrate. A boy named Francisco, for example, would celebrate on the Feast of St. Francis, which is October 4. Name days were once a larger celebration than a birthday, but are now becoming less common.

CELEBRATIONS AND HOLIDAYS

January 1 **New Year's Day**

First Monday in February **Constitution Day**

Third Monday in March **Birthday of Benito Juárez**

Friday before Easter **Good Friday**

May 1 **Labor Day**

May 5 **Anniversary of the Battle of Puebla** *(Cinco de Mayo)*

September 16 **Independence Day**

October 12 *Día de la Raza*

November 1 and 2 *Día de los Muertos*

Third Monday in November **Revolution Day**

December 12 **Day of our Lady of Guadalupe**

December 25 **Christmas Day**

ACTIVITY

Mexican markets are filled with skulls in October. Mexicans often make and decorate sugar skulls, or *calaveras de azucar*, at home. They place the skulls on *Día de los Muertos* altars or on gravestones. These skulls have been a tradition since the 1600s. They are to remind us of the circle of life and honor those who have died. These attractive objects come in all sizes and are brightly decorated. Sometimes, people write the name of a departed loved one on the skull's forehead.

To make these skulls you will need a mold, which is easy to buy online or at craft stores. Have an adult help you find the molds, and don't use the oven or a mixer without adult help!

You can buy icing instead of making it, but it may not dry as hard as the Royal Icing recipe and your skulls might not last as long. Make sure not to buy "gel" icing since that will never harden.

EQUIPMENT:

double-sided skull mold
pastry or icing bags, or Ziploc bags (just fill with icing and cut the tip of one corner out to squeeze)
mixing bowls
whisk, or stand mixer
small piece of cardboard

FOR DECORATIONS:

Chiclets
Tic Tacs
sunflower seeds
sugar pearls
sprinkles
colored foil or sequins
gems and rhinestones
glitter
ribbons
feathers
beads
fake flowers
anything else you can think of!

FOR SUGAR SKULLS:

6 cups sugar
2 egg whites

FOR ICING:

2 cups confectioner's sugar
4–5 teaspoons water
4 teaspoons light corn syrup
1 teaspoon lemon juice
gel food coloring

INSTRUCTIONS FOR SKULLS:

1. Mix ingredients in a bowl until it feels like wet sand.
2. Pack into molds firmly, overfilling them.
3. Use cardboard to scrape excess off the top to flatten the surface.
4. Put cardboard on top and flip the mold over.
5. Lift off the mold and leave the skull on the cardboard.
6. Repeat for the back of the skull.
7. Place in the oven at 200°F (93°C) for 30 minutes to harden.
8. Glue front and back pieces together with icing, using your finger to wipe off excess from the edges.
9. Decorate!

INSTRUCTIONS FOR ICING:

10. Mix confectioner's sugar and water in a glass bowl until smooth.
11. Start with less water and only add more if it's too thick. Mix the lumps out!
12. Add light corn syrup and mix fully.
13. Stir in lemon juice and mix fully.
14. Divide the icing into bowls. Add gel food coloring to each bowl and mix. Use immediately, or store for up to three days in an airtight container with a piece of plastic wrap on the surface. Stir before using.

INSTRUCTIONS FOR DECORATING:

15. You don't need to use glue—the icing is your glue. First, make eyes, nose, and teeth, then decorate any way you want! You can use icing to make any design you can think of. Squiggles, zig zags, hearts, dots, flowers, stars… hair, glasses, or hats. You can also use icing to stick objects to the skull: sequins for eyes, Chiclets or Tic Tacs for hair, or anything that will stick just for decoration!

Visitors from Italy taught the people of Mexico sugar art in the 1600s, but the symbolism of skulls goes back thousands of years.

Each family builds its own Day of the Dead altar, called an ofrenda.

Día de los Muertos, like many holidays in Mexico, gains its special flavor from the blending of Catholic religion and pre-Columbian rituals. Families build altars for departed family members and decorate their gravestones. They make offerings of food and drinks that the deceased enjoyed and eat skull-shaped foods. There are large parades too, with people in elaborate costumes. Two million people attended Mexico City's parade in 2018. This holiday celebrates ancestors and accepts death as a natural part of life.

Other holidays honor Mexico's freedom and *mestizo* heritage. For example, Columbus Day is celebrated as *Día de la Raza* ("Race Day") in recognition of the *mestizo* aspects of the country and because Mexicans do not want to pay respect to the colonizing Europeans.

Many Mexicans follow ancient traditions, such as Aztec celebratory body painting.

Fiesta de Quince Años

The *Fiesta de Quince Años*, or *quinceañera*, is a rite of passage for Mexican girls as they turn 15. This celebration started in indigenous cultures. It was adapted to European Catholic traditions. The *Fiesta* begins with a special Mass and ends with a party where girls wear beautiful ballgowns and tiaras.

There are an estimated 63 to 82 million mestizos in Mexico.

Over 80 percent of Mexico's people are Catholic. However, the country recognizes freedom of religion. Like the United States, Mexico is a secular country. This means they practice separation of church and state.

The country's large indigenous and *mestizo* population blend Catholicism with traditional religions. In *fiestas*, ancestors and spirits are honored along with Catholic saints. Also, saints have taken on the features of traditional spirits.

CHAPTER 5

WHAT'S FOR DINNER?

Mexico's incredible cuisine comes from both indigenous and European food. Famous dishes like tamales and tacos have their roots in ancient foods but were changed using European techniques and ingredients.

Many ingredients important to Mexico's modern cuisine are native to the area. Corn, chile peppers, tomatoes, and beans are just some of the indigenous ingredients now familiar to people worldwide.

The comal *is a large griddle used to cook traditional Mexican dishes.*

Chile peppers are hung to dry in bunches called ristras.

Mexicans usually eat four meals. *Desayuno* is a light breakfast, and *almuerzo* is similar to our brunch—but they eat it every day! *Comida*, or lunch, is the largest meal of the day, while *cena*, or dinner, is the lightest. Snacks, called *botanas*, are popular and sold by street vendors.

Chiles, vanilla, and chocolate are some of the special flavors that make Mexican cuisine great. Chocolate is part of even savory dishes, like rich *mole* sauce. Chocolate for drinking is made from cocoa and spices, sometimes even chiles! This combination was an ancient Aztec favorite.

Common dishes in Mexico are tostadas, soft-shell tacos, *tortas* (sandwiches), stuffed chiles, and quesadillas. These foods might be familiar, but what about corn fungus or grasshoppers? These are some of the foods eaten by Mexicans that are uncommon for foreign diners.

In parts of Mexico, fish is grilled with vegetables and achiote, a red-colored spice with a smoky, pepper-like flavor.

Mayans traditionally make tortillas by hand using a *comal* over an open flame.

There is a special way of making Mexico's most famous food, tortillas. First, a small stone table called a *metate* is used to grind the corn. It is then prepared using a unique method called nixtamalization (can you see the word *tamal* in there?), where it's soaked and softened with limewater or lye. This allows corn to hold together in a dough (called *masa*) and tortillas to be formed.

Three Sisters

Maize, beans, and squash are the three main crops of indigenous Americans, including those in Mexico. They are known as the Three Sisters because they helped each other grow when planted together. They are still some of the most common foods in the country. Together they form a well-rounded diet.

RECIPE

Want to taste a snack that many Mexican kids enjoy? Try this simple recipe that serves four. Ask an adult to help you with any slicing or chopping.

Bright, bold flavors such as the ones found in this dish are a common characteristic of many Mexican foods. Next time, try replacing the cucumbers in this recipe with carrots or a root called jicama. Then share this Mexican street snack with friends and family.

INGREDIENTS:

- 4 small cucumbers
- 4 limes
- 1 tablespoon (17 grams) salt
- chile powder (to taste)

INSTRUCTIONS:

1. Store the cucumbers in the refrigerator until chilled. Have an adult use a knife to carefully cut the cucumbers into thin slices.
2. Place the cucumber slices in a bowl.
3. Squeeze the limes over the slices in the bowl.
4. Sprinkle the cucumber slices with the salt and chile powder.
5. Using tongs, mix the cucumbers, lime juice, salt, and chile powder.
6. Allow the cucumbers to sit for 5 minutes.
7. 7. Put the cucumbers on plates. If you like, you can add another light sprinkling of salt and chile powder before serving. Enjoy!

Taco stands, or *taquerias*, are everywhere in Mexico. Street vendors are common too. *Fondas* are restaurants that only open for *comida*. They serve a set menu with soup, rice, beans, tortillas, and a main dish.

One taqueria *taco usually costs between 25 cents and $1.*

Mexicans begin meals by saying *provecho*, meaning *enjoy*! Even other diners at a *fonda* might say it to you as they pass. It's a sign of the country's welcoming nature. Won't you go and tell them *provecho* too?

Tamales

Cornmeal tamales are a filled dumpling, steamed inside corn husks or banana leaves. They are time-consuming to make, so they are a special holiday food for Mexicans and Mexican Americans too. They are cooked in huge batches at parties called *tamaladas*.

GLOSSARY

cartels *(kahr-TELS)* a combination of businesses that try to control prices

colonized *(KOL-uh-nayhz-d)* a country or nation that is controlled by another country

deforestation *(DEE-for-ihs-tay-shun)* the removal of trees and forests for human use

ecotourism *(EE-koh-tor-iz-uhm)* when people visit a new place to enjoy its natural beauty in a respectful way

epidemics *(e-puh-DEM-ik)* disease outbreaks that harm a great many people

exports *(EK-spohrts)* goods that leave one country when they are sold to another country

habitat loss *(HAB-ih-tat LOS)* the destruction of land where animals live or plants grow, often from human activity

heritage *(HAYR-uh-tij)* something that is handed down from the past

imports *(IM-pohrts)* goods that are brought into a country after they are purchased from another country

indigenous *(en-DIJ-en-uhs)* people native to a specific area

industrialization *(in-DUHSS-tree-uhl-eye-ZAY-shun)* the start of big business and factories in a specific city, country, or region

latitude *(LAT-ih-tood)* a distance north or south of the equator, measured in degrees

legislative *(LEJ-is-ley-tiv)* related to the branch of government that makes laws

livestock *(LAYHV-stok)* animals that are raised on a farm or ranch

missionaries *(MISH-uh-nahr-ees)* people who are sent by a church into another area to explain or convert people to their religion

petroleum *(puh-TROH-lee-uhm)* oil that is taken from the earth and used to make gasoline and other products

pre-Columbian *(PRE-koh-LUM-bee-uhn)* existing in North, Central, or South America before the arrival of Columbus in 1492.

temperate *(TEM-pur-ett)* having mild weather without extreme hot or cold seasons

FOR MORE INFORMATION

BOOKS

Orr, Tamra. *Mexican Heritage.* Celebrating Diversity in My Classroom. Ann Arbor, MI: Cherry Lake Publishing, 2018.

Tonatiuh, Duncan. *Danza!: Amalia Hernández and el Ballet Folklórico de Mexico.* New York: Abrams Books for Young Readers, 2017.

Williams, Brian. *Maya, Incas, and Aztecs.* DK Findout! New York: DK Publishing, 2018.

WEB SITES

DLTK's Sites—Mexican Recipes
https://www.dltk-kids.com/world/mexico/recipes.htm
Try your hand at Mexican cooking, from Mexican hot chocolate to tacos.

National Geographic Kids—Mexico
https://kids.nationalgeographic.com/explore/countries/mexico
Explore facts on the geography, culture, and history of Mexico.

Rockalingua—Learning Spanish
https://rockalingua.com/videos
Learn the basics of Spanish with a variety of music videos.

INDEX

ABOUT THE AUTHOR

Leah Kaminski loves international travel. She especially likes learning about the culture and ecology of other countries. Leah lives with her husband and baby boy in Chicago, where she teaches, writes poetry, and writes books like this one.